Cool as a Cucumber!

For Joe who always did like his broccoli!

First published in paperback in 2005 by Zero To Ten,
a division of Evans Brothers Ltd, 2A Portman Mansions,
Chiltern St, London W1U 6NR

Publisher: Anna McQuinn
Art Director: Tim Foster
Senior Editor: Simona Sideri
Publishing Assistant: Vikram Parashar

A CIP catalogue record for this book is available from the British Library.

ISBN 1-84089-414-8

Copyright © 2002 Zero to Ten Limited
Photographs copyright © 2002 Sally Smallwood

Printed in China

Picture credits
A-Z Botanical Collection: potatoes, green pepper; Holt Studios: radish,
peas, avocado, mushroom; Photos Horticultural: cucumber, celery.

Sally Smallwood

Cool as a Cucumber!

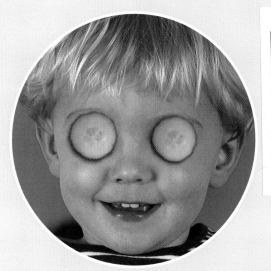

potatoes

often different like...

pasta

sweet potato

rice

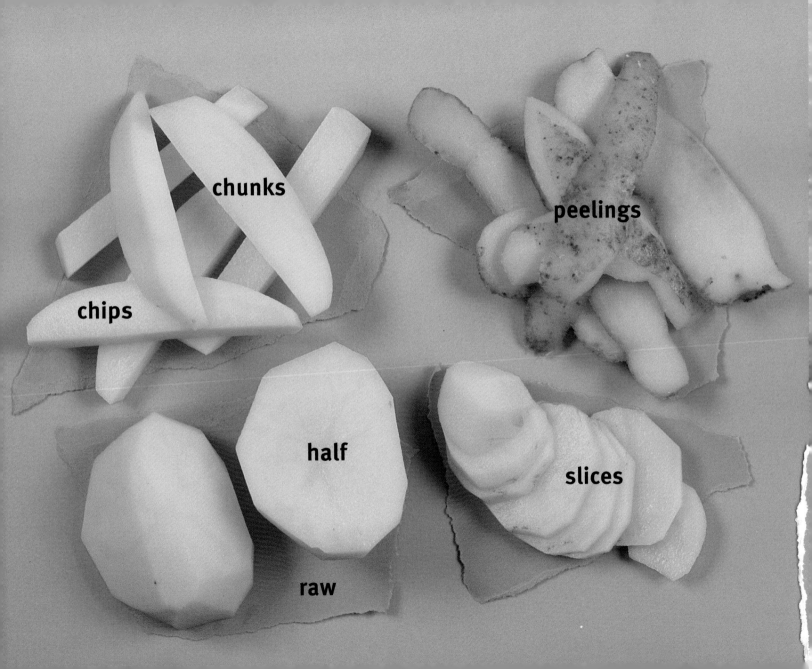

chunks

chips

peelings

half

slices

raw

radish

leaf

skin

skin

stalk

half

root

slices

cucumber

cool and refreshing like...

yoghurt

beansprouts

grapes

peas

avocado

bumpy skin

stone

half

pulp

half

smooth

soft

stone

green
pepper

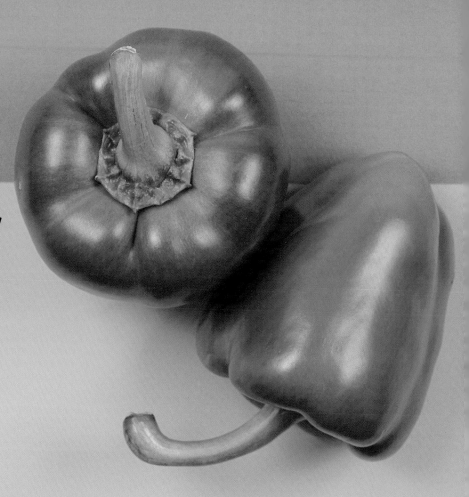

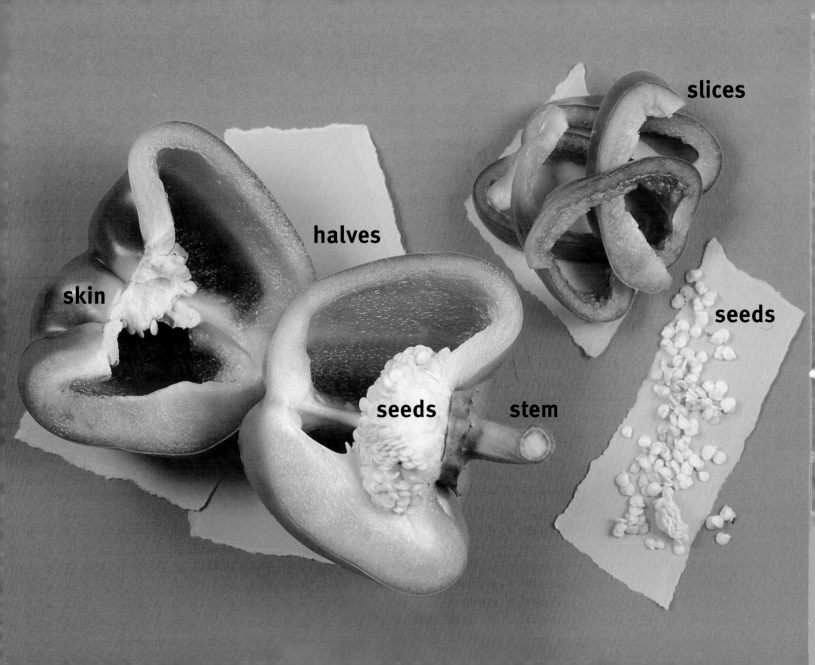

slices

halves

skin

seeds

stem

seeds

celery

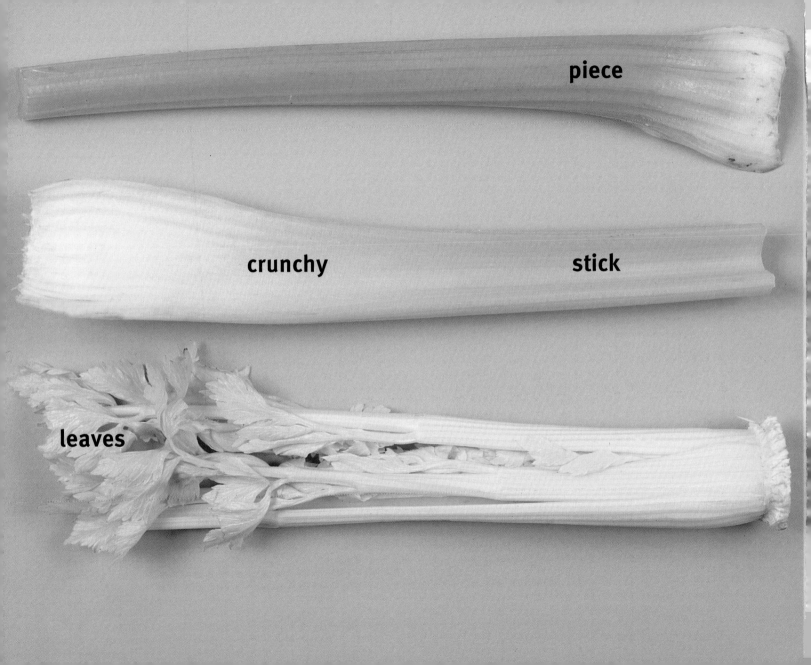

piece

crunchy

stick

leaves

mushroom

soft and slippy like...

avocado

pasta

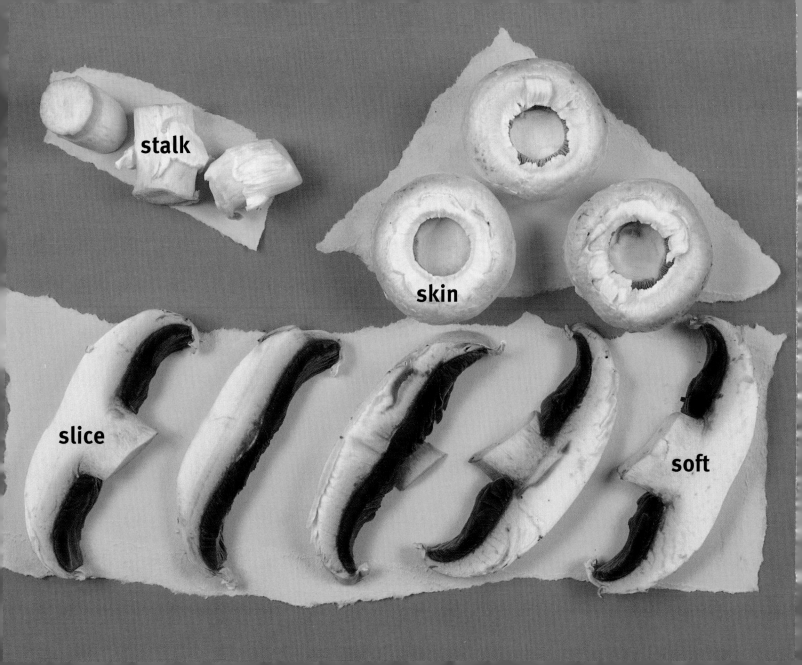